Animal World

THE KANGAROO

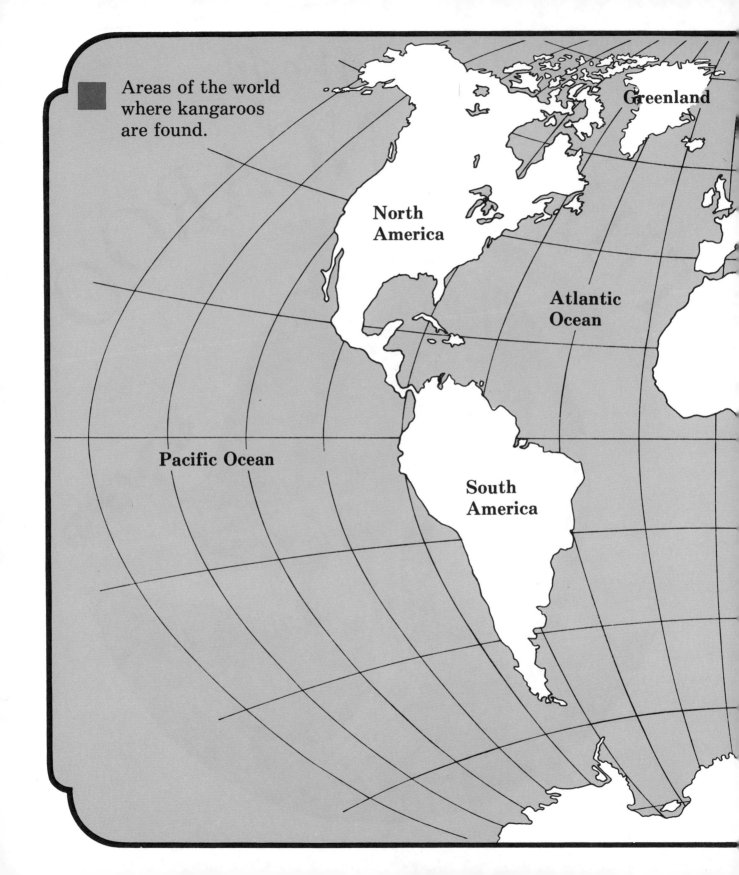

Areas of the world where kangaroos are found.

Greenland

North America

Atlantic Ocean

Pacific Ocean

South America

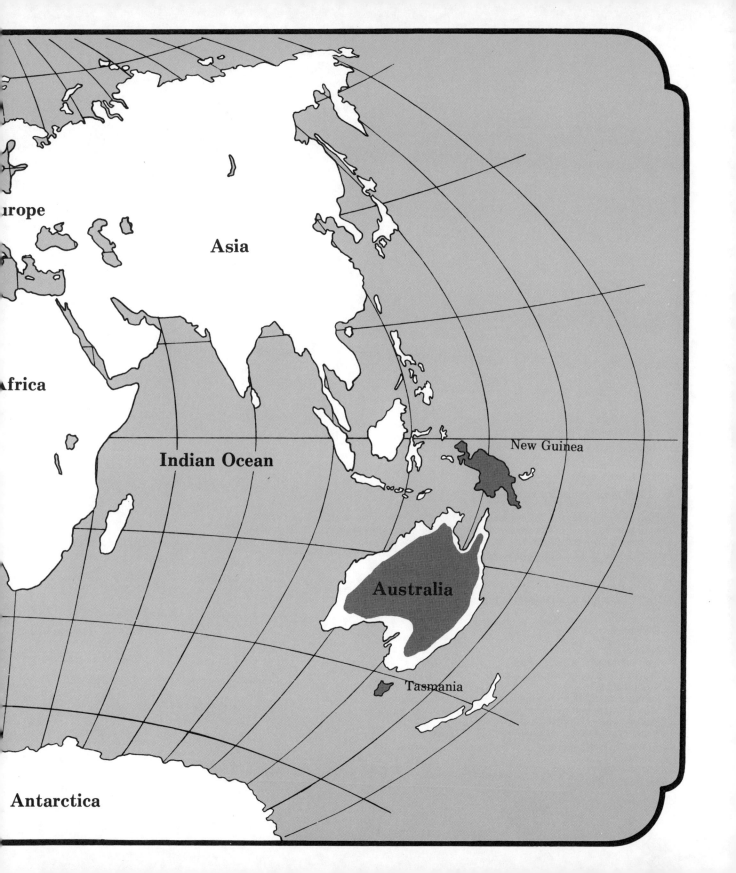

Year 2000 home library edition

Published by The Rourke Enterprises, Inc., P.O. Box 3328, Vero Beach, Florida 32964.
Copyright ©1983 by The Rourke Enterprises, Inc. All copyrights reserved. No part of this
book may be reproduced in any form without written permission from the publisher.
Printed in the United States of America.

Library of Congress Cataloging in Publication Data

Dalmais, Anne-Marie, 1954-
  The kangaroo.

  (Animal world)
  Translation of: Le Kangourou.
  Reprint. Originally published: London : Macdonald
Educational, 1978.
  Summary: Describes the natural environment, physical
characteristics, and behavior of the kangaroo, focusing
on the red kangaroo of Australia.
  1. Red kangaroo — Juvenile literature.   [1. Red
kangaroo.   2. Kangaroos]   I. Giannini, ill.   II. Title.
III. Series.
QL737.M35D3413   1984   599.2   83-9749
ISBN 0-86592-864-9

Animal World

THE KANGAROO

illustrated by
Giannini

This edition produced
exclusively for
A+ Child Development, Ltd.

ROURKE ENTERPRISES, INC.
Vero Beach, FL 32964

On the Australian plain

Here is a hot, sunny plain in Australia. It is very flat
and stretches far into the distance. The gum trees have
narrow leaves and only give a little shade to the baking
earth. A koala bear is clinging to the trunk of a gum
tree. A kind of anteater called a numbat is nosing
around for ants in the roots of the grass.

Suddenly, three kangaroos come bounding along
behind the trees.

A family at rest

Not far from the gum trees, a kangaroo family has
stopped for a rest. The father is stretched out on his
side. He is nearly six and a half feet long. He has long
ears and a soft, woolly coat. He is reddish-brown and
grey in color. His hindlegs are much bigger than his
forelegs and have very strong muscles for jumping.

The mother is standing nearby. She is a smoky grey
color. She is carrying a baby in her pouch. He is called a
joey. All you can see of him here is his little head.

Always on the move

Kangaroos do not have a fixed home. They are always
on the move, travelling at night when it is cool.

During the day they rest because it is hot. This family
is taking shelter from the sun in a cool cave.

Food for the joey

While the joey is in the pouch he lives on milk from his mother. As he gets older, he is able to lean out of the pouch and nibble plants. This joey is being watched by a cockatoo and some budgerigars.

Food for the adult kangaroos

Kangaroos eat plants of many kinds. They are called "herbivores" or plant eaters. Here you can see the mother kangaroo feeding. Her tail helps her to balance.

Four large emus and their three little chicks are standing close by. These birds can run fast and are good swimmers, but they are not able to fly. They are curious about the kangaroos, so they do not run away.

Kangaroos can go without drinking for two or three months. To do this they must spend the days resting, and eat fresh plants at night.

The kangaroo's jump

Kangaroos can cover as much as thirty three feet in one jump. They use their powerful tails to spring off. Their tails also help to keep them steady.

As his parents bound along, the joey stays out of sight. His mother gave him a gentle tap on the head to make him get well down inside her pouch.

A mob of kangaroos

Kangaroos like to have company. They often travel in large groups, called mobs. The leader of each mob is an older male. He keeps all the kangaroos together.

When the mob stops to rest, one of the kangaroos always stays on guard. He warns the others if there is any sign of danger. The kangaroo is usually silent. To give the alarm signal he coughs noisily and drums the ground with his hindlegs.

The joey leaves the pouch

When winter comes, the kangaroo mobs move to the drier regions of Australia.

The joey is now seven months old.
He has grown much bigger and he
no longer lives in his mother's
pouch. Now, he feeds on plants
like an adult. He jumps around
with the other kangaroos in the
mob. As you can see, he still
takes milk from his mother.

The young kangaroo is curious. Here, he leaves the mob in order to study a flock of sheep. They are all standing around a sheep station. Should he feel frightened, however, he will rush back to the mob.

SOME INTERESTING FACTS ABOUT KANGAROOS

Species:

Two hundred years ago few people outside Australia had ever seen a kangaroo. It is believed that the name for this animal came from an English explorer, Captain James Cook. He saw a group of them while traveling through Australia in 1770.

Kangaroos are mammals and marsupials. A mammal is a species of animal in which the babies are born live and feed on their mother's milk. A marsupial is a pouched animal.

There are about 55 species of kangaroos and wallabies. They are found in Australia, New Guinea and Tasmania.

Close cousins of kangaroos and wallabies are koalas, Tasmanian wolves, Tasmanian devils and American opossums. The American opossum is the only marsupial which lives outside Australia.

The animals on the previous page (starting at the right corner and moving clockwise) are: the tree kangaroo, the wombat and the bandicoot. All live in Australia.

Description:

The animals of Australia are different from anywhere else in the world. This is because Australia is an island continent. The animals there have developed without interbreeding with other animals. In other parts of the world, marsupials died out when non-pouched animals dominated them. This is not true in Australia. There they have thrived almost without enemies.

Many years ago a giant kangaroo lived in Australia. It stood about 10 feet tall. No kangaroo alive today is that large. The average is 5 feet 6 inches.

There are two main types of kangaroos. The grey or forester is the one described in this book. It lives in the wetter areas of forests. The red kangaroo lives in the drier areas and on the plains. An adult male weighs about 150 pounds. However, old red males can run to 200 pounds. Small kangaroos are hardly bigger than rats. In fact, one of this type is called the rat kangaroo. Middle sized kangaroos are pademelons, wallabies and wallaroos.

The brain of a marsupial is smaller than that of other mammals, compared to its body size. This may be one reason why they were not able to compete in other parts of the world. The average adult is between 3 and 5 feet tall and weighs 88 to 154 pounds. The tail can run 31 to 39 inches.

The hindlegs are very strong. They are long and well muscled. A kangaroo can jump 25 feet across and 10 feet high. It can run at speeds of 25 to 30 miles per hour. When a female kangaroo is carrying her joey she must be careful that he does not fall out when she runs. So, when she is about to leap, she taps him lightly on the head. He ducks in the pouch. Strong muscles close the flap opening and the baby is safe.

There are 2 or 3 toes on the hind foot. They are covered by one layer of skin. The kangaroo uses them to groom his fur.

Their front paws are also powerful. They are much shorter than the hindlegs. When in danger the kangaroo will hold them up, like a boxer. It also fights like a boxer. Its punch is very strong. It can easily kill a small animal, or seriously hurt a man. Like most animals, the kangaroo does not look for a fight. But it will fight if it thinks that there is real danger.

Kangaroos are herbivorous. That means that they eat only plants. The average kangaroo in the wild can expect to live about 20 years.

Family Life:

The word "marsupial" comes from the Latin "marsupium" meaning "pouch." A marsupial is any animal where the female of the species has a pouch. Most pouched animals live in Australia.

The reason that the female has a pouch has to do with the way that the babies are born and develop. The gestation period for kangaroos is between 8 and 40 days, depending on the species. Gestation is the time that the baby grows inside its mother's body before it is born. After such a short time the embryo (baby) is very underdeveloped. It could not survive in the world if it were left on its own. Immediately after birth it quickly climbs inside the pouch that the mother has on the front of her body. There it will be fed with her milk. It will be warm and safe until it is old enough to live outside. This takes about 7 months.

The birth process in kangaroos is a fascinating thing to watch. A kangaroo has one baby or "joey" at a time. The baby is very tiny. It measures one inch long. Its eyes are closed and its ears are not developed. The tail is a mere stump, as are the legs. Its mouth is a hole. The only part that looks fairly well developed is the front paws. There is a reason for this. As soon as it is born it must get into the pouch. If it does not reach the pouch soon, it will die. The front paws are used for this. It climbs by instinct through its mother's fur to reach her pouch. The mother will lick a path through to help but the baby must find the way all by himself.

Having jumped in the pouch, the joey must now find a nipple. He takes milk from it. He never lets the nipple go until he is old enough to survive for a while without it. This means that he has developed eyes, ears, legs and fur. He is now a strong, kicking baby. Now he is curious. He loosens his hold on the nipple and peeks outside the pouch for the very first time in his life. When he is about three months old he will feel sure enough to hop outside the pouch. He will stay out for only a few minutes though. When in danger he will jump back in.

A herd of kangaroos is called a "mob." There are about 12 individuals in a mob. Males, females and joeys all live together. The Australians called red kangaroo males "boomers." The females are called "blue flyers."

Most kangaroos live on the ground, leading the life of a nomad. However, a few live in trees. Two of these types live in northeast Australia. They are called "boongaries." Physically they differ from their cousins in that they have hooked claws. These are very useful in climbing trees. They have been seen leaping very far from branch to branch.

Conservation:

Australia is still unpopulated over vast regions. These areas are where the kangaroos live. As men continue to take over this land, the kangaroo population will suffer. This has been true of other animals in the past.

"I Love Mom and
From Arabella